To my twin niece and nephew, born into a strange world
which they will no doubt make better
Ali

To Zélie and Lucia
Mickaël

First published in the United Kingdom in 2021 by Lantana Publishing Ltd., Oxford.
www.lantanapublishing.com | info@lantanapublishing.com

American edition published in 2021 by Lantana Publishing Ltd., UK.

Text © Ali Winter, 2021
Illustration © Mickaël El Fathi, 2021

Distributed in the United States and Canada by Lerner Publishing Group, Inc.
241 First Avenue North, Minneapolis, MN 55401 U.S.A.
For reading levels and more information, look for this title at www.lernerbooks.com
Cataloging-in-Publication Data Available.

Printed and bound in China
Original artwork created with mixed media, completed digitally

Hardcover ISBN: 978-1-911373-71-1
PDF eBook ISBN: 978-1-911373-74-2
Trade ePub3 ISBN: 978-1-913747-63-3
S&L ePub3 ISBN: 978-1-913747-48-0

SCIENCE AND ME

ALI WINTER . MICKAËL EL FATHI

Lantana

ALFRED NOBEL and the Nobel Prize

Alfred Nobel grew up in Sweden dreaming of inventions. His father was a skilled engineer and taught him the basics of engineering from an early age. Alfred particularly loved learning about how things get blown up: in other words, explosives.

When Alfred's family moved to Russia during the Crimean war, Alfred and his father became very interested in a new explosive liquid called "nitroglycerin." No one had yet worked out how to handle nitroglycerin safely. It was a lot more powerful than gunpowder and liable to explode unexpectedly.

Turning the family kitchen into a laboratory for his experiments, Alfred discovered that a special mixture of nitroglycerin and gunpowder could be blown up safely. Alfred called this mixture "dynamite." He tested it out by setting off explosions on a frozen river outside Saint Petersburg.

Although dynamite was very useful in building projects, it was also very destructive. It would cause untold damage if used in war so, instead, Alfred secretly hoped that it would lay the foundation for world peace. Sadly, his prophecy didn't come true. Dynamite became a weapon.

As he lay on his deathbed at the age of sixty-three, Alfred felt a strange combination of regret mixed with pride in his achievements. He decided to donate most of his large fortune towards five annual prizes in Physics, Chemistry, Medicine, Literature, and Peace.

Alfred hoped that by rewarding the best ideas and inventions, he could make amends for the weapon of war he had accidentally unleashed on the world.

Read on to discover some of the extraordinary men and women who have been awarded Nobel Prizes in Physics, Chemistry, and Medicine. Find out how their brilliant discoveries have shaped the world around us.

Alfred Nobel (1833-1896) created five Nobel Prizes. They have been awarded annually (with some exceptions) since 1901.

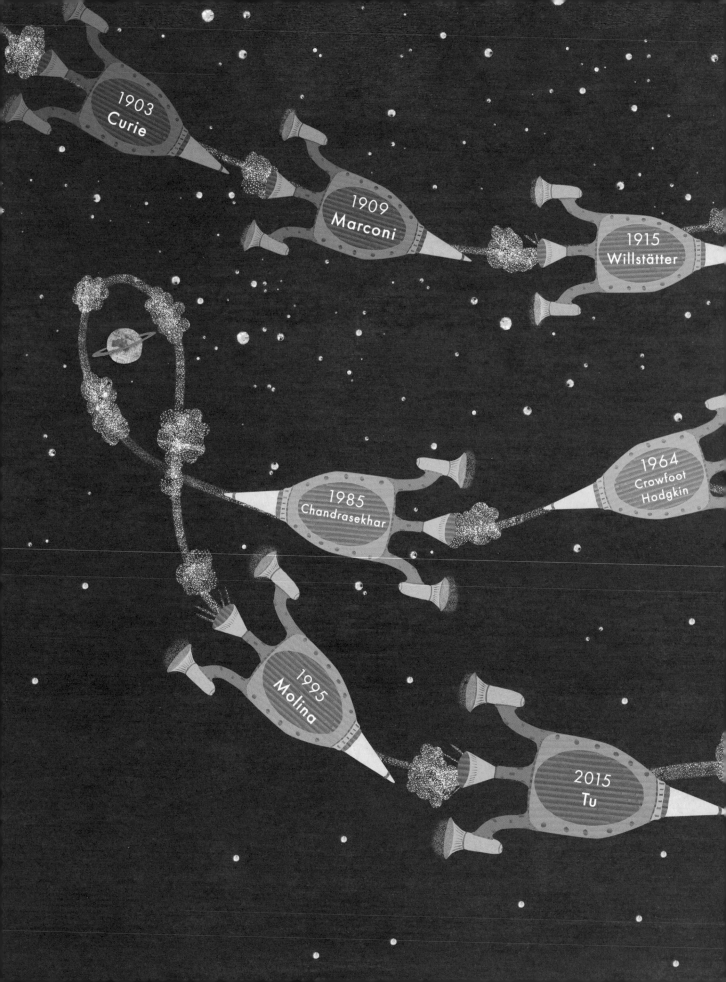

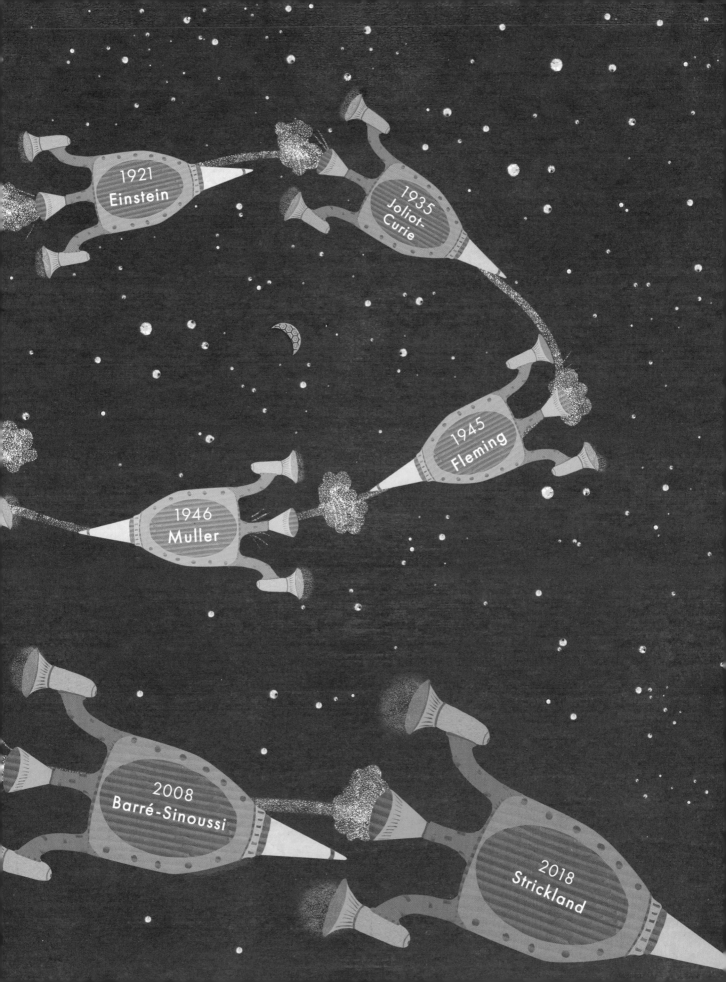

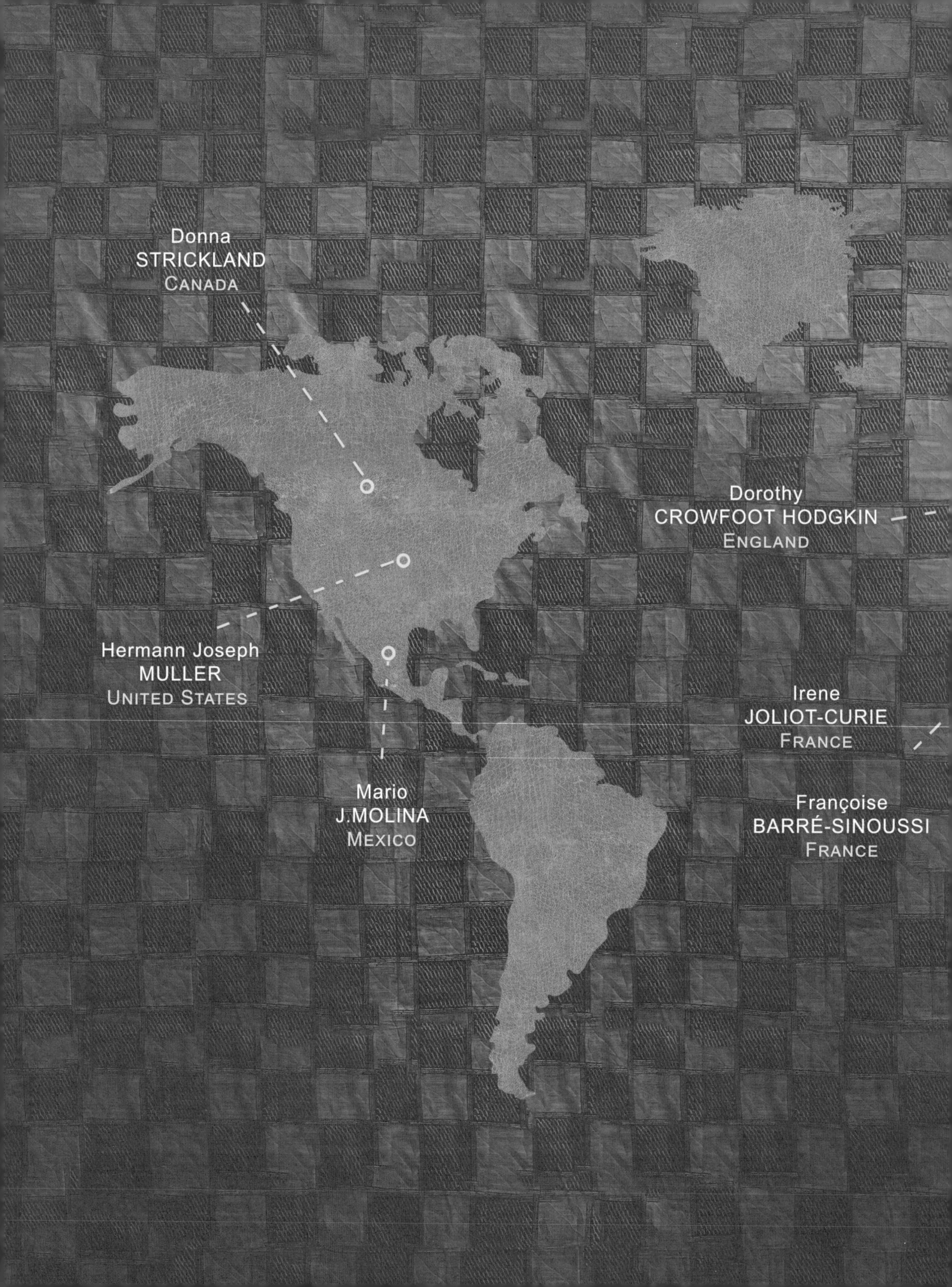

Donna
STRICKLAND
CANADA

Dorothy
CROWFOOT HODGKIN
ENGLAND

Hermann Joseph
MULLER
UNITED STATES

Irene
JOLIOT-CURIE
FRANCE

Mario
J.MOLINA
MEXICO

Françoise
BARRÉ-SINOUSSI
FRANCE

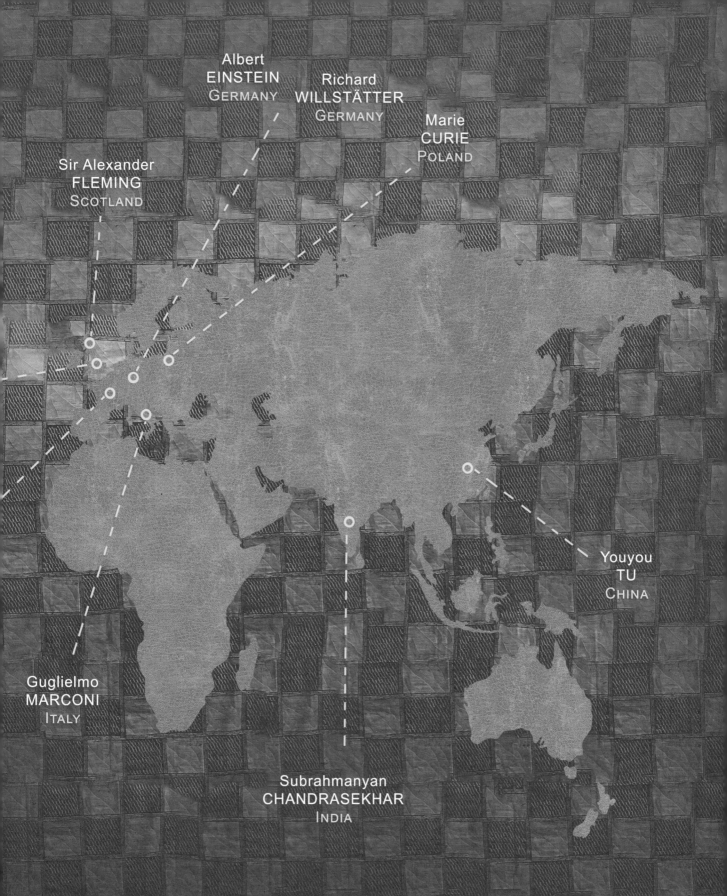

Albert
EINSTEIN
GERMANY

Richard
WILLSTÄTTER
GERMANY

Marie
CURIE
POLAND

Sir Alexander
FLEMING
SCOTLAND

Youyou
TU
CHINA

Guglielmo
MARCONI
ITALY

Subrahmanyan
CHANDRASEKHAR
INDIA

Science is...giving us hope

Inspired by the discoveries of...Marie Curie

and Irene Joliot-Curie

The fact that Maria Skłodowska was a woman put her at a disadvantage. Growing up in Poland in the late 19th-century, she couldn't earn a degree at the University of Warsaw. She had to study in secret at Warsaw's unofficial "floating university," where classes were held at night in changing locations to avoid detection by the police.

At the age of twenty-four, Maria moved to Paris where she could study physics and mathematics. There, she met a man named Pierre Curie who was equally passionate about science. They married, and together, Maria—now known as **Marie Curie**—and Pierre made an exciting discovery: two new radioactive elements they named "polonium" and "radium."

Marie and Pierre's daughter, Irene, was born at the turn of the century. As she grew into a young woman, Irene began helping her mother in the laboratory. There, she met Frédéric Joliot, and the two scientists later married. **Irene Joliot-Curie** and Frédéric Joliot discovered how to manufacture radioactive atoms artificially. This breakthrough changed the course of modern science.

As well as being brilliant researchers, Marie and Irene showed their heroism during World War I. Distressed by the terrible human suffering, the mother-and-daughter team worked as battlefield nurses. Marie designed special vans fitted with X-ray machines that became known as "Petite Curies." Both women risked their lives driving the vans to the frontline where they examined wounded soldiers for broken bones.

Marie was the first woman to win a Nobel Prize, and the first scientist to win Nobel Prizes in both Physics and Chemistry. She remains the only person in history to have won a Nobel Prize in two different scientific fields. Twenty-four years after her mother won the Nobel Prize in Chemistry, Irene was awarded the same.

Tragically, neither Marie nor her daughter knew how dangerous radioactive elements could be, and both died of radiation poisoning before they reached old age. Their lives were short, but their vital contribution to science lives on.

Marie Curie (1867-1934) won the Nobel Prize in Physics in 1903 and in Chemistry in 1911

Irene Joliot-Curie (1897-1956) won the Nobel Prize in Chemistry in 1935

Science is...staying in touch

Inspired by the discoveries of Guglielmo Marconi

Guglielmo Marconi had always had an inventive spirit. He was intrigued by radio waves, which most people thought were nothing more than a kind of invisible light. Guglielmo had other ideas. At the age of twenty, he began his own tests with radio equipment. Soon, he was able to send signals a short distance to a receiver. With this single homemade experiment, the spark of wireless communication was born.

Excited by his invention, Guglielmo wrote a letter to the Ministry of Post and Telegraphs in Italy in the hope that they would fund his work. But the Director was unimpressed.

Guglielmo was not ready to give up so he journeyed to London, where the Chief Electrical Engineer of the British Post Office saw potential in the new device. There, Guglielmo perfected his radio. In 1910, he sent a signal all the way from Ireland to Argentina—a distance of over 6,000 miles, or the length of around two million cars lined up bumper to bumper!

The radio offered more than simply a new way of sending information. It turned out to be life-saving. In 1912, hundreds of people were rescued at sea when *RMS Titanic* hit an iceberg and sank beneath the waves. Thanks to Guglielmo's radio, rescue ships were able to find the stranded lifeboats and return survivors to shore.

Today, Guglielmo is remembered as the man whose invention laid the foundation for future radio technology, the basis of the mobile phones we use today.

Guglielmo Marconi
(1874-1937) won the Nobel
Prize in Physics in 1909

Science is...refusing to do harm

Inspired by the discoveries of...

Richard Willstätter

Richard Willstätter was always eager to learn. As a boy, he collected stamps, coins, and minerals, and conducted chemistry experiments in his uncle's factory in Germany.

As an adult, Richard's most promising investigations delved deep into plant life. Richard studied how plants produce "chlorophyll:" the pigment that turns their leaves green and helps them convert sunlight and water into food. His experiments transformed our understanding of how plants grow.

Richard's discoveries helped him find a job teaching at a German university, and he was working there when World War I was declared. A group of scientists asked him to help Germany make poisonous gases for use in the war, but Richard refused. Instead, he designed masks and clothing to protect people from the gases these scientists were developing.

After the war, Richard experienced increasing prejudice against Jewish people. When a colleague made an anti-Semitic comment during a meeting, Richard walked out. He never returned to the university, and he left Germany for good just before the outbreak of World War II. He lived the remainder of his life in Switzerland.

Richard's protest sent a powerful message to the scientific community. He chose to take a stand against intolerance in the face of powerful opposition.

Richard Willstätter (1872-1942) won the Nobel Prize in Chemistry in 1915

Although **Albert Einstein** would grow up to become one of the most famous physicists of all time, he didn't have a promising start. He failed many of his classes at school and was told by his teachers that he wouldn't amount to anything.

But that didn't dampen Albert's spirits. Looking back on his childhood in Germany, he saw that two "wonders" set him on the path to becoming a scientist: a compass he was given at the age of five, and a book of geometry he received at the age of twelve. Albert was fascinated by the invisible forces that made the compass needle move, and by the properties of light beams.

Albert struggled to find a job at a university. But this didn't stop him from writing four academic papers in what is now known as his "miracle year" of 1905. These papers shook up everything physicists knew about light, matter, mass and energy, and time.

At first, the papers were ignored by the scientific community. But luckily, one influential scientist, Max Planck, saw how brilliant Albert's theories were. Max gave him a chance to talk about his work to scientists around the world. From there, Albert's fame soared.

Yet, back home, Germany was becoming increasingly hostile to Jewish people. The German government began publicly burning Albert's books, and in 1932, Albert fled Germany for America, never to return.

Albert was a lifelong pacifist. He championed the civil rights movement of the 1950s and 60s, and called for an end to racial discrimination. He spent the rest of his career trying to discover an ultimate "theory of everything." This idea still fascinates scientists to this day.

Inspired by the discoveries of

Albert Einstein

Albert Einstein (1879-1955)
won the Nobel Prize in
Physics in 1921

Science is...learning from our mistakes

Inspired by the discoveries of Sir Alexander Fleming

Alexander Fleming spent his early life deep in the Scottish countryside. Every day, he walked four miles to school and four miles back again. Spending this time outdoors helped him develop a love of the natural world, from the beauty of the forests to the fascinating plants underfoot.

As he grew up, Alexander turned his attention from nature to the body. He began studying bacteria, and particularly the micro-organisms that can cause disease.

In 1928, by chance, he left the window open in his laboratory when he went away on a trip. When he returned, he found a strange substance on his samples. To Alexander's amazement, this substance had stopped harmful bacteria from growing. He named the antibiotic "penicillin." It was a medicine that would save millions of lives in the years to come, and is still used by doctors today.

But this wasn't Alexander's only accidental achievement. During World War I, he had found to his dismay that the chemical antiseptic nurses were using to treat soldiers' wounds in fact killed white blood cells. These are the very cells that fight off disease. In many cases, antiseptic was doing more harm than good. After the war, while he was looking for a better alternative, Alexander sneezed into his samples and found that his mucus destroyed bacteria. He had chanced upon the body's own natural antiseptic that defends us against disease.

Luck had a big part to play in both of Alexander's discoveries. But without his inquisitive eye and scientific intuition, they might have passed him by.

Sir Alexander Fleming (1881-1955) won the Nobel Prize in Medicine in 1945

It was important to **Hermann Joseph Muller**'s parents that their son should respect everyone, no matter their background. These values stayed with Hermann for life.

Growing up in the United States, Hermann was fascinated by science, and set up a science club at school to perform daring experiments. At university, he studied genetics: the science of how living things pass their characteristics on to their offspring.

Hermann knew that when genes change, or mutate, these changes can be passed on to the next generation. Hermann found a way to alter genes artificially using X-rays. This in itself was an important development for science, but Hermann had in fact stumbled upon something even more momentous. He had discovered the dangers of radiation, which can cause mutations and cancers inside people's bodies.

As the years passed, Hermann began to worry a great deal about how radiation from nuclear weapons testing was harming men and women across the globe. Already, two great scientists—Marie Curie and Irene Joliot-Curie—had died from cancers caused by radiation. Two cities in Japan, Hiroshima and Nagasaki, had been destroyed by nuclear weapons with a devastating loss of life. The issue was urgent.

In 1958, Hermann and many of his fellow scientists signed a letter addressed to the United Nations calling for an end to nuclear weapons testing.

Just as Alfred Nobel had understood the power of scientific discovery to cause great harm as well as great good, Hermann felt it was his duty as a scientist to consider the human cost of his achievements.

Hermann Joseph Muller (1890-1967) won the Nobel Prize in Medicine in 1946

Dorothy Crowfoot Hodgkin
(1910-1994) won the Nobel
Prize in Chemistry in 1964

Inspired by the discoveries of **Dorothy Crowfoot Hodgkin**

For the first four years of her life, lived in Egypt. When her family moved back to England, Dorothy was full of curiosity, and passionate in particular about crystals. She was one of only two girls allowed to study chemistry at school, a subject thought "only for boys."

When she grew up and began working as a tutor in natural sciences at the University of Oxford, Dorothy was asked to figure out the structure of penicillin, the antibiotic discovered a few years earlier by Sir Alexander Fleming. The work would require investigating atoms: the building blocks of molecules. As the tiniest units of every chemical, atoms are far too small for us to see with the naked eye. Dorothy found them fascinating. Using X-rays, she discovered the three-dimensional shape of many atoms, helping us understand how the smallest pieces of nature fit together.

Such detailed scientific research was not easy for Dorothy. From a young age, she had been diagnosed with arthritis, a painful condition that made it difficult for her to move her hands and feet. She did not let this deter her. Nor did she forget her early childhood in Africa, and she spent much of her life championing scientists around the world who had fewer resources than she did.

Yet, despite all these achievements, when Dorothy was awarded the Nobel Prize in 1964, a newspaper headline read: "Housewife wins Nobel Prize." The newspaper conveniently forgot to mention that Dorothy was a member of the Royal Society and a ground-breaking scientist! Thankfully, today, her intelligence and determination do not go uncelebrated.

Science is...expanding our horizons

Subrahmanyan Chandrasekhar, known as Chandra to his friends, spent his childhood in India with his nine brothers and sisters. His gift for science was undeniable from an early age. He began a physics degree when he was only fourteen years old, and was then awarded a scholarship to study at the University of Cambridge in England.

Chandra had always been fascinated by stars. Scientists used to think that all stars eventually became "white dwarfs." These are old stars that have used up all their fuel and become very dense and not nearly as bright as younger stars. But Chandra felt certain that there was more to discover.

In 1930, while on board the boat to England that would take him to his new university, Chandra calculated a special number: 1.44. He discovered that stars with a mass more than 1.44 times that of our sun eventually explode and can leave behind a "black hole" —a region in space where gravity is so strong that not even light can escape it.

Using mathematics, Chandra had answered one of the greatest mysteries of the universe. But an older scientist named Sir Arthur Eddington did not agree with his theory. Unfortunately for Chandra, Arthur was so well-known that most people took Arthur's side. Even Chandra's friends, who knew he had made a brilliant discovery, refused to support him in public. It would take several decades before the evidence for black holes became so overwhelming that the world gave Chandra the recognition he deserved.

So when we look up at the night sky, we can thank Chandra for persisting in what he knew was right, even if he had to wait a long time for the rest of the world to believe him.

Subrahmanyan Chandrasekhar (1910-1995)
won the Nobel Prize in Physics in 1983

Inspired by the discoveries of Subrahmanyan Chandrasekhar

Science is...thinking of our children

Mario J. Molina's interest in chemistry was sparked when he looked into a toy microscope for the first time. Soon, he was turning the bathroom of his home in Mexico into his own little laboratory.

In the early 1970s, after studying in several countries, Mario grew interested in chemicals called "chlorofluorocarbons" (CFCs). Most people thought that CFCs were harmless, and they were widely used in products like hairsprays and refrigerators. But Mario was worried.

He wondered what would happen when pollution from CFCs built up in the atmosphere. Working with his colleagues, he discovered that CFCs in large quantities, high in the earth's atmosphere, can damage the ozone layer. The ozone layer works like a shield wrapped around the earth, letting in light but keeping out harmful radiation from the sun. The more the ozone layer is destroyed, the worse global warming will become.

Mario and his team alerted other scientists, politicians, and journalists to their discovery. They were determined that the world should not turn its back on such a global problem. Many people did not believe them.

Eventually, a hole was found in the ozone layer above the Antarctic. It proved that Mario had been right all along. Every country in the world then passed laws to ban the use of CFCs, and the global community came together to take a step forward in protecting our environment.

In 2013, Mario was awarded the Presidential Medal of Freedom by then US president Barack Obama because of his courage, persistence, and foresight.

Mario J. Molina (1943-)
won the Nobel Prize in
Chemistry in 1995

Inspired by the discoveries of Mario J. Molina

Science is...calming our fears

As a child, Françoise Barré-Sinoussi spent her summers in the French countryside where even the tiniest insect could capture her attention for hours. Although she felt drawn to medicine, she chose to study natural sciences at university because the course was more affordable. She knew her family had little money to spare.

While Françoise was working at a laboratory in Paris, reports of a new disease began circulating. The disease was named Acquired Immune Deficiency Syndrome (AIDS), and people were frightened because nobody understood the cause.

Françoise discovered that AIDS was caused by a virus named Human Immunodeficiency Virus (HIV). Her findings marked a huge breakthrough for patients because they helped doctors develop life-saving treatments. Françoise and her team at the university gave those living with AIDS something incredible: the promise of a future.

Françoise never lost sight of the painful human impact of the disease. She spent hours with patients in hospitals—something scientists rarely did. She even journeyed to the Central African Republic and Vietnam, two of the countries worst affected. For Françoise, tackling the disease was as much a personal mission as it was a team effort by scientists.

Even now, Françoise insists that the fight against AIDS isn't over. She is determined to discover a total cure. Through her deep empathy for others, this extraordinary scientist has given the world much to be hopeful for.

Françoise Barré-Sinoussi (1947-) won the Nobel Prize in Medicine in 2008

Inspired by the discoveries of

Françoise Barré-Sinoussi

Science is...making sure nothing is forgotten

Winning a Nobel Prize in Medicine without any kind of medical degree may seem like an impossible feat. But for one woman from China, the impossible became a reality.

When **Youyou Tu** was sixteen, she became very ill with an infection called tuberculosis. After putting her studies on hold for two years, Youyou recovered her health and decided to devote her life to medical research.

During her time as a young scientist, malaria—a disease spread by mosquitoes—was becoming an increasing global problem. Countless scientists before her had failed to find a cure. But in the late 1960s, when the Chinese government asked her to investigate, Youyou took on the challenge with determination.

Youyou was inspired by both Western and traditional Chinese medicines. She set about poring over more than 500 ancient medical texts—some dating back over 3,000 years—to search for a cure. She found a glimmer of hope in one of these ancient books. It mentioned "Qinghao," the Chinese name for the herbs in the Artemisia family, from which you can extract "Artemisinin." Demonstrating complete dedication, Youyou tested the drug on herself to see if it was safe to use.

Her commitment paid off: the treatment was a success. Artemisinin has since saved over two hundred million lives around the world. But despite her incredible triumph, Youyou's work did not receive international recognition until the 1980s. Now, Youyou is celebrated for her astounding ingenuity, when others had given up the fight.

Youyou Tu (1930-) won the Nobel Prize in Medicine in 2015

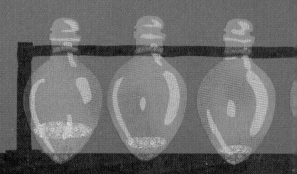

Inspired by the discoveries of Youyou Tu

Science is...seeing the world differently

Inspired by the discoveries of...

Donna Strickland

When **Donna Strickland** was ten years old, her family took a trip to the Ontario Science Centre in Toronto, Canada. There was a large laser on display. "You'll want to see this," Donna's father said. "Lasers are the future." Strong, focused beams of light: lasers represented the cutting edge of science. Donna was instantly hooked.

When she grew up and studied engineering physics at university, Donna was excited to find that lasers were part of the course. After graduation, her supervisor asked her to work out how to make the lasers' light beams

stronger and more intense. The first experiment she tried failed, but she persevered. After many long hours, she finally cracked it. Donna was thrilled.

Her discovery increased the intensity of the laser light so much that it now had many uses, from glass cutting to eye surgery. Common eye conditions such as near-sightedness, far-sightedness, and astigmatism could all be treated with Donna's laser.

But Donna's career might never have happened if she had listened to the teachers who told her that mathematics and science were "boys' subjects." Throughout her studies, she had few female classmates and not a single female professor.

When she was woken by a phone call early one morning in 2018 and the voice on the other end of the line told her that she had won the Nobel Prize in Physics, she thought it was a cruel joke. But it wasn't a joke. She was the first woman in 55 years to win the prize, and only the third female physics laureate.

Donna Strickland (1959-) won the Nobel Prize in Physics in 2018

SCIENCE IS...

...giving us hope
...staying in touch
...refusing to do harm
...believing in a better world
...learning from our mistakes
...foreseeing danger
...persisting against the odds
...expanding our horizons
...thinking of our children
...calming our fears
...making sure nothing is forgotten
...seeing the world differently

WHAT DOES SCIENCE MEAN TO YOU?